Winters Rest

Majestic Reflection
Devotional Study Series - Book One

A quarterly devotional by:

J. K. Sanchez

Winters Rest: Book 1 of Majestic Reflection Devotional Study Series.
ISBN -13: 978-0692323106
ISBN – 10: 0692323104.
Copyright © 2014 by J. K. Sanchez.
Published by: Button Lane Books Spanaway, WA 98387

Contact: Judy@jksanchez.com - www.jksanchez.com

Cover Photography by:
Majestic Reflection-J.K.Sanchez Photography
Cover Design by:
Turtleshell Press www.turtleshellpress.com

Dedication

To those who have begun and continue to walk on this narrow path of simplification, rest and stepping into a life journey of pursuing the presence of our Lord Jesus Christ above all other life distractions.

Contents

<u>Acknowledgments</u>

As I contemplate this section of gratitude I am overwhelmed with the many friends and family that through encouragement, teaching, and directing have brought me to the beginning of this new adventure. To you all I am forever grateful.

First and foremost, I am thankful and blessed by the love of my husband, Dennis who is and always will be my best friend and love of my life and to my children: Amber, David and Daniel who have always made life full of joy. To you my family a huge thank you for all your patience that has allowed me to freely walk and grow in this "winters rest" process.

To my friend, my sister in Christ – Pat, I am eternally thankful for your love and example of Christ that was poured into a young mini skirt teen. You taught me what it truly means to love Jesus with all my heart and to develop a foundation of prayer that has established me in a strong faith and walk in Christ.

With love and gratitude to my friend and mentor; Evie who taught me who I am in Christ – Your example poured into me the love of His presence and that special <u>knowing</u> deep within that "I am His Beloved". Your passion was contagious and developed an insatiable fire within me. I know that there is nothing more important then to sit in the presence of the Holy Spirit thanks to your direction.

I offer a huge thank-you to my friend Cherrie who inspired this book with a simple request to write out my thoughts.

The publishing process involves a huge learning curve; this curve was smoothed out for me by two new friends who openhandedly answered my many questions. Elizabeth Parker – Author and Nick Thacker – Author - you both were a breath of fresh air and I am thankful for your willingness to help.

My love, appreciation and gratitude are eternally given to my sister, my cheerleader, my friend, my almost TWIN in every way and <u>my editor</u>. Thank you Donna for always being there and knowing my thoughts before I speak them.

And finally – but above all – my thanks to Jesus Christ who directed, inspired, taught me (step by step) how to **rest** in His presence and who continually opens doors of His favor and abundance over my life.

My life is not my own but a gift freely given back to the one who gave His life for me.

Introduction

My passionate journey for the presence of the Lord began within me decades ago and has drawn me to a narrow path filled with promise and freedom that I have never experienced before. During this journey I have found a deep <u>knowing</u> of my true identity as a daughter of the King and His amazing love for ME. As my path has narrowed to a place of the <u>one thing</u> – His face and presence - I have learned a new depth of rest, new life, joy and the importance of simplification that has brought me the true freedom of Christ.

His gift on the cross is just that – a gift. All of the "I can do's" are learning to lie down as my life is becoming focused on Him and what has already been "done" for me.

This book series has been ignited directly from that love and I desire to share, direct and encourage you to a place to meet Him, love Him, hear Him, see Him and be a lover of His presence as I am.

Most devotionals are 365 days of amazing deep thoughts that honestly, most of us don't make through. We miss a few days and give it up.

This devotional study series is:

Based on a **quarter** and a 6-day week; (leaving day 7 for you to experience the filling of His presence as you gather with others).

It is **perpetual** so it can be used year after year as you walk out this journey.

It is **interactive** – it gives you a comparatively thought filled piece of writing and then builds with scripture and questions that will stir you to look deep within yourself - making this a personal growth experience.

ENJOY THIS AMAZING JOURNEY TO FINDING REST AT HIS FEET!

Taking New Territory

Each time you begin a new year, a new job, a new relationship etc. you have been given an opportunity to walk into new territory. A whole new place in which you can expect to see dreams fulfilled, long awaited changes to occur and promises come to pass.

During the colonial enterprises, the Samurai would often plant a cherry blossom tree to symbolize a victory where territory was taken.

Your new beginning has sprung forth with expectation of territory to be won.

The past is gone.

Your victory has been won as you accept the undeserved gift purchased for you on the cross of Jesus Christ.

Your choice is simply to accept that gift (your planted Cherry Tree) and leave the past failures and hurts behind. This victory then allows you to freely walk into your new territory with expectation of new fulfillment of promises.

Join me and step with victory out of past failure into all that He has planned for you. Plant your cherry blossom tree and take that new territory.

Day 1

Spend some time contemplating what *Taking New Territory* means to you.

1. What does this mean to you?

2. How does it apply to your life?

Day 2

John 3:16 - For God so loved the world, that he gave his only Son, that whoever believes in him should not perish but have eternal life.

I John 1:9 - If we confess our sins, he is faithful and just to forgive us our sins and to cleanse us from all unrighteousness.

Acts 4:12 - And there is salvation in no one else, for there is no other name under heaven given among men by which we must be saved.

This free gift that Jesus paid for was undeserved and unearned.

1. Have you accepted His free gift?

Whether you have just today accepted this free gift* or you have known Christ for many years; contemplate that gift and the victory it has brought to your life.

2. What does His gift of salvation mean in your life today?

*(Accepting Jesus is simply acknowledging your sin and need for forgiveness. Asking Him to forgive you and believing He died for you, that he forgives you, loves you and has the very best in store for you. It's that simple. Welcome to the Kingdom of God!)

Day 3

A new year = a new slate! Your past is gone.
Journaling – writing down your thoughts, frustrations, God conversations, questions, desires, dreams and beyond is an important discipline to all areas of growth in our lives. This devotional will encourage that thought process. So write, write and write. Get a separate journal notebook and be prolific in your thoughts. Amazing things jump from the Holy Spirit out on to the page as we express ourselves.

2 Corinthians 5:17 - Therefore, if anyone is in Christ, he is a new creation. The old has passed away; behold, the new has come.

1. What will you write on that new slate?

2. What are those lost dreams, unspoken ideas, or buried promises?

Day 4

I Peter 2:16 - Live as people who are free, not using your freedom as a cover-up for evil, but living as servants of God.

Galatians 5:1 - For freedom Christ has set us free; stand firm therefore, and do not submit again to a yoke of slavery.

As you read and contemplate these two scriptures allow them to stir up personal meaning.

1. What does it mean to be "free" in Christ?

2. How can you apply these to your life situation and walk in a new freedom today?

Day 5

2 Peter 1:3-4 - His divine power has granted to us all things that pertain to life and godliness, through the knowledge of him who called us to his own glory and excellence, by which he has granted to us his precious and very great promises, so that through them you may become partakers of the divine nature, having escaped from the corruption that is in the world because of sinful desire.

Today take some time and study on a few of the promises of God. Find one that specifically speaks to you and your life right now.

1. What promise can you take hold of and believe for your life today?

Day 6

Re-read *Taking New Territory*.

Psalm 37:4 - Delight yourself in the Lord, and he will give you the desires of your heart.

1. What desires has God begun to stir in your heart?

2. What past dreams have been laid down but are being rekindled?

3. What symbol has God placed in your heart to symbolize the taking of new territory for this year?

Step out and in the victory purchased at the cross move into a new territory filled with dreams and promises fulfilled.

You are victorious through Jesus Christ!

Desire for a Single Drop of New Wine

With the desire for just a single drop of new wine comes the understanding that there is a process of change that must occur.

The old wine skin with its past taste and presence of old wine must be cast off to allow a new supple skin to be prepared.

With desire comes acceptance and anticipation of this new wine. The joy that will come from that one drop of wine as it touches your tongue stirs within. All the past doesn't compare to that desire, making the cast off process an easy choice.

This new skin is now ready to receive, expand and contract as the new flavor begins. An amazing fragrance begins to bubble up from within - allowing the fermentation to occur.

The sweetness of this coming new wine continues the maturing process as it rests, breathing in and out allowing pressure to grow and release.

The excitement of a new sweet taste begins to grow, along with an aroma that is beginning to swirl within. Excitement and anticipation begin to erupt within this new wine skin as the wine changes and is ready to be poured out.

The time to taste has arrived and with it comes a cry of exhilaration from your heart.

Your heart sings out "Just one single drop is more than enough"

But the skin bulging with fragrant sweetness has done its work and pours forth a release within you that erupts in a joy of transformation as the new wine saturates not only you but also the very atmosphere that surrounds you.

Join me as you begin to desire the exciting changes to come - the casting off of old wineskins as well as a renewed hunger and thirst for more of His presence.

Day 1

Spend some time contemplating what *Desire for a Single Drop of New Wine* means to you.

1. What does this mean to you?

2. How does it apply to your life?

Day 2

The Holy Spirit fills us with new wine through new revelations and understanding of the scriptures as well as His manifest presence on a daily basis. Our old wineskins can be old ways of thinking, past experiences and our preconceived acceptance of life. Inside each of us dwells a desire for understanding, experiencing and seeing more of who God is. The Holy Spirit living within makes that possible.

2 Corinthians 3:18 - And we all, with unveiled face, beholding the glory of the Lord, are being transformed into the same image from one degree of glory to another. For this comes from the Lord who is the Spirit

Romans 12:2 - Do not be conformed to this world, but be transformed by the renewal of your mind, that by testing you may discern what is the will of God, what is good and acceptable and perfect.

As you have read and contemplated the last two scriptures - allow them to stir up personal meaning.

1. What two areas of your life do you feel you have allowed yourself to be conformed to this world?

2. What choices can you make today to begin to allow the Spirit of God to transform those areas?

Day 3

With the desire for new wine comes the stirring of changes being applied to your life.
Being willing for that change is a choice that allows that desire to spring forth.

Psalm 51:10 - Create in me a clean heart, O God, and renew a right spirit within me.

1. What choices can you make today that will make room for changes to take place?

Day 4

Psalm 42:2 - My soul thirsts for God, for the living God....

Psalm 63:1 - O God, you are my God; earnestly I seek you; my soul thirsts for you; my flesh faints for you, as in a dry and weary land where there is no water.

1. What does thirsting for God look like to you?

2. How would you express that?

Spend some time in prayer asking the Holy Spirit to stir up your desire for new wine.

Day 5

Matthew 9:17 - Neither is new wine put into old wineskins. If it is, the skins burst and the wine is spilled and the skins are destroyed. But new wine is put into fresh wineskins, and so both are preserved.

1. How would you express the desire level for this type of new wine in your life right now?

2. Have you seen ways this week to stir that desire up? How can you apply that stirring to your life?

Day 6

Re-read *Desire for a Single Drop of New Wine.*

1. How has your desire for a deeper walk with Jesus been stirred this week?

2. Apply something new today to your personal relationship with Christ. (A few suggestions: Sing, Dance, Pray, Read, Take a walk and just talk to Him, Sit in silence just listening.)

   Journal your experience and thoughts of your time spent with the Lord today.

ENJOY HIS NEW WINE EVERY DAY.
You are highly favored!

<u>Blanket of Peaceful Purity</u>

Snowflakes begin to fall and with them amazing change appears. They start to build up and bring quietness to the air. Accumulating they begin to lay a blanket over the landscape. This silent white blanket of flakes brings a peace and contentment that settles over the entire atmosphere.

Where barrenness, clutter, filth and decay may have once reigned only moments before now a pure blanket lies quietly upon them, covering the once chaotic scene. Before your eyes the change occurs and these changes bring change within your own spirit. Peace falls - contentment begins to find home and rest reigns, even if for a short time.

Often there are parallels between nature and the spiritual.

As I contemplate the quiet scene that is materializing and the change of atmosphere before me I see how barrenness, clutter, filth and decay are carried within.

If you open your heart and allow access to Jesus, He will bring purity like the snow. When He comes you are promised not a covering of all your decay that will melt away but a complete obliteration of your internal decay that will change the atmosphere in you and around you.

When that obliteration comes the amazing gift of the Holy Spirit comes in like a flood – cleansing and changing you. The permanent promise of peace, contentment, rest and freedom materializes in your life as you walk in His presence through Christ.

Just as nature responds with acceptance of this blanket of peaceful purity you too can accept the free gift of His forgiveness to obliterate your decay and walk in a place of peace, forever at rest.

<u>Day 1</u>

Spend some time contemplating what *Blanket of Peaceful Purity* means to you.

1. What does this mean to you?

2. How does it apply to your life?

Day 2

Opening the door for Jesus allows Him to bring peace into our life. We can enjoy that peace every day as we walk in the true identity of a forgiven child and finding freedom to go in and out of His pasture.

John 10:9 - I am the door. If anyone enters by me, he will be saved and will go in and out and find pasture.

I Thessalonians 5:23-24 - Now may the God of peace himself sanctify you completely, and may your whole spirit and soul and body be kept blameless at the coming of our Lord Jesus Christ. He who calls you is faithful; he will surely do it.

1. Explain your understanding of your personal identity in Christ.

Day 3

Philippians 4:7 - And the peace of God, which surpasses all understanding, will guard your hearts and minds in Christ Jesus.

1. Does peace and contentment reign in your life or do you find areas of barrenness, clutter, decay and filth?

Those areas of "yuck" in your life no longer need to have authority to rule. Understand that the blood of Christ has obliterated them.

Spend some time today allowing His presence to reign in your life. Pass those areas of "yuck" under His blood and walk in peace.

Winters Rest

Day 4

Isaiah 32:17 - And the effect of righteousness will be peace, and the result of righteousness, quietness and trust forever.

1. What does this scripture say to you?

2. How can you apply that today?

Day 5

Romans 15:13 - May the God of hope fill you with all joy and peace in believing, so that by the power of the Holy Spirit you may abound in hope.

1. How would you describe the atmosphere of your environment both internal and external?

2. Does the knowledge of freedom through Christ give you joy and hope?

Spend time enjoying that hope and watch your environment change.

Day 6

Re-read *Blanket of Peaceful Purity*.

1. What "yucky" area have you been able to see obliterated this week, as you placed it under the blood of Christ?

2. Spend some time today in thankfulness for His forgiveness and grace through Jesus Christ.

You are forgiven!

The Deep Roots of Victorious Conquerors

As I sit silently absorbing the beauty of the trees around me I am drawn once more into contemplation of the enormity of my Heavenly Fathers creative design.

The most interesting thought and spiritual parallel is found in the very roots beneath these trees, of which we never see but without them they could never complete the plan and design that God had created them for.

The trees that are the strongest, those who weather the toughest storms and produce the most fruit have strong deep roots.

Deep roots are pursued in the quite unseen places of the earth. They are made stronger over years of endurance as they press down through soil, clay and rock searching for the deep water.

Those that find the deep water gain refreshment while others are withering. These are those that survive the droughts of heat-parched ground and survive the strongest winds that pound and bend them almost to the ground. Here they continue to stand tall, solid and are ready to fight the next battle.

These are the same that stand as the strongest towers, the front lines of the storms. They stand as protectors and guards for many others.

These tenacious towers find strength from the deep water beneath. Their roots support and hold strong to that unseen faith in the position of their taproot. They continually draw from the deep unseen river.

Our understanding and continual revelation of Jesus Christ as our taproot determines our root system, our trees purpose and plan and the ability to stand as one with deep roots. We can be one who comes through the battle victorious - still standing as a conqueror.

It's that deep unseen root system and faith that will allow this tree to grow to its full purpose.

Day 1

Spend some time contemplating what _The Deep Roots of Victorious Conquerors_ means to you.

1. What does this mean to you?

2. How does it apply to your life?

Day 2

It's faith in the unseen promises of Christ that give us strength. Pressing through the soil, clay and rock bring endurance as well as the solid "I know He has my back" knowing that dwells deep inside.

Hebrews 11:1-3 - Now faith is the assurance of things hoped for, the conviction of things not seen. For by it the people of old received their commendation. By faith we understand that the universe was created by the word of God, so that what is seen was not made out of things that are visible.

1. What events in your life have strengthened your faith in Christ?

Day 3

Those who have loved you through Christ and who have stood beside you, encouraged and cheered you on are all part of that intricate network of roots.

Ephesians 3:14-19 - For this reason I bow my knees before the Father, from whom every family in heaven and on earth is named, that according to the riches of his glory he may grant you to be strengthened with power through his Spirit in your inner being, so that Christ may dwell in your hearts through faith—that you, being rooted and grounded in love, may have strength to comprehend with all the saints what is the breadth and length and height and depth, and to know the love of Christ that surpasses knowledge, that you may be filled with all the fullness of God.

1. Who are the people in your life that have encouraged and helped your roots to grow?

The need for mentors in your life never is complete.
We are also never to young to reach out to love and mentor another.

2. Consider those that are around you currently; is there someone that you would like to receive strength from? Step out and talk to them about that.

3. Ask the Holy Spirit to direct you to someone that may need a little extra encouragement or love today.

Day 4

I Corinthians 15:57 - But thanks be to God, who gives us the victory through our Lord Jesus Christ.

Romans 8:37 - No, in all these things we are more than conquerors through him who loved us.

1. What is and where do you find **deep** water?

2. How can you dig deeper today to reach the waters that bring true refreshment?

Spend time today with Jesus. Allow a thankful heart to well up from deep inside. For we are victorious in Christ Jesus!

<u>Day 5</u>

Jeremiah 17:8 - He is like a tree planted by water, that sends out its roots by the stream, and does not fear when heat comes, for its leaves remain green, and is not anxious in the year of drought, for it does not cease to bear fruit.

1. As you reach deep, what revelation of your purpose in Christ has He shown you?

2. What types of fruit (character) have begun to bud in your life this month?

Day 6

Re-read *The Deep Roots of Victorious Conquerors.*

1. What new revelation from God did you receive this week as you spent time in His presence?

2. Can you apply this directly to your daily life? If so - where can it be applied and how can you achieve it?

3. Take time today in thankfulness for the victory that belongs to us because of the love of Christ poured out on the cross.

You are a child of the KING!

His Creative Forces

We all walk in a world of pressure imposed on us from our circumstances, others demands and internal unfulfilled expectations. How we respond to those pressures can cause us to grow and become like that beautiful life giving waterfall or the destructive force of a volcano.

In nature pressure also does both; creates beauty or destruction - pearls, diamonds and waterfalls as well as earthquakes and volcanoes.

Pearls and diamonds are created in a place of pressure where stillness and time are the Creator's force. Waterfalls are created from a constant movement to a place of freedom that erupts with the joyful sound of release.

Just like the creative force behind the pearl and diamond we can walk through pressures <u>resting</u> in the knowledge that through Christ "He's got our back" - and with that comes a freedom and joyful release of pressures like the waterfall.

Walking through daily pressures in this way will create a thing of beauty and transform you from "glory to glory".

It's your choice what you want those pressures to create - beauty or destruction.

Day 1

Spend some time contemplating what *His Creative Forces* means to you.

1. What does this mean to you?

2. How does it apply to your life?

Day 2

Romans 8:5 - For those who live according to the flesh set their minds on the things of the flesh, but those who live according to the Spirit set their minds on the things of the Spirit.

1. How do you currently walk through pressure imposed on you in your daily life?

2. Thinking of a destructive reaction you may have expressed recently - write out an example of how you could have reacted differently?

Day 3

Ezekiel 36:26 - And I will give you a new heart, and a new spirit I will put within you. And I will remove the heart of stone from your flesh and give you a heart of flesh.

Proverbs 17:22 - A joyful heart is good medicine, but a crushed spirit dries up the bones.

1. Contemplate the differences you see in the creation of pearls and diamonds versus earthquakes and volcanoes.

2. Where do you see destructive forces under pressure reigning in your life?

3. Where are the forces of beauty under pressure reigning in your life?

Day 4

Psalm 37:7 - Be still before the LORD and wait patiently for him; fret not yourself over the one who prospers in his way, over the man who carries out evil devices!

Philippians 4:7 - And the peace of God, which surpasses all understanding, will guard your hearts and your minds in Christ Jesus.

1. List at least 2 ways that you believe these two scriptures could change how you might react to a current stressful situation in your life.

2. Endeavor to apply them today as you walk through your day.

Day 5

Learning to be still and wait on God is a decision that will always bring about peace, contentment, beauty and joy. It will produce diamonds and pearls within your character - it's a choice.

Proverbs 4:26 - Ponder the path of your feet; then all your ways will be sure.

Psalm 46:10 - Be still and know that I Am God. I will be exalted among the nations, I will be exalted in the earth!

1. Take time today to "Be Still". Listen to His voice and express your understanding of these two scriptures as they currently apply to your life.

Day 6

Re-read *His Creative Forces*.

Isaiah 55.12 - For you shall go out in joy and be led forth in peace; the mountains and the hills before you shall break forth into singing, and all the trees of the field shall clap their hands.

In Christ we are free (completely forgiven) of old reactions, even those done minutes ago. Trusting in His undeserved grace in our lives brings life. His presence brings desire for change. Sitting at His feet will produce the constant movement toward freedom and joy - just as the waterfall cascades to freedom over the precipice.

> 1. How have the changes you have made this week changed your life and your atmosphere?

> 2. Take time today to rejoice in the free gift of His undeserved favor that reigns over your life.

3. Journal any thoughts that the Holy Spirit began to stir as you contemplated the meaning of that free gift.

You are redeemed!

The Choice – To Mount Up with Wings like Eagles

The majestic Eagle depends on his physical design; strength, speed and sharp vision for his survival. Just as the Eagle does, so do we often depend on the "I" of our abilities.

There comes a time to the Eagle where a molting process must be faced. This process brings this majestic proud bird to a weakened position. His feathers, strength, vision and ability to fly or hunt are eliminated during this time of preparation for renewal.

We too, come to this place; where all of what "I" can do and what "I" have done are no longer of value. We then face a choice, a choice of the heart. A choice that requires a willingness to give up all of what "I" can do and trust in what "He" did for us at the cross.

The Eagles too must make a similar choice. Many roll over and die choosing the memory of the "I" of their former majesty. Those who are renewed are those who turn to the sun, rest and wait. They then are restored not to the former majesty but to a stronger and greater one.

We too can only reach new heights with renewed vision and strength when our eyes are on the "Son" not the "I". Only then can His plans, purposes and design for our life be renewed.

Trust that His plans for you are far greater then your "I" plans. So chose today to learn from the renewed Eagle. Join me and look to the Son - Rest and Wait.

<u>Day 1</u>

Spend some time contemplating what <u>*The Choice – To Mount Up with Wings like Eagle*</u> means to you.

1. What does this mean to you?

2. How does it apply to your life?

Day 2

I Peter 5: 6-7 - Humble yourselves, therefore, under the mighty hand of God so that at the proper time he may exalt you, casting all your anxieties on him, because he cares for you.

1. What area of your life do you see the "I" working hard?

2. Take time today to go to the throne of grace and lay that "I" at His feet.

Day 3

Luke 12:27 - Consider the lilies, how they grow: they neither toil nor spin, yet I tell you, even Solomon in all his glory was not arrayed like one of these.

1. Consider the difference between the effortless flight of the eagle and a flock of busy "flapping" birds. Which best describes you?

2. How can you apply the eagle lifestyle to your current situations?

Day 4

Psalm 103:2-5 - Bless the LORD, O my soul, and forget not all his benefits, who forgives all your iniquity, who heals all your diseases, who redeems your life from the pit, who crowns you with steadfast love and mercy, who satisfies you with good so that your youth is renewed like the eagle's.

1. As you waited on the Lord this week - what things did He reveal to you that might need to be laid down – allowing Him to take over?

2. How can you begin to apply them?

Day 5

Isaiah 40:31 – but they who wait for the Lord shall renew their strength; they shall mount up with wings like eagles; they shall run and not be weary; they shall walk and not faint.

1. Where do you feel renewal beginning to stir?

2. What would this scripture mean to you if everything you currently do changed and was done as He directed?

Day 6

Re-read _The Choice – To Mount Up with Wings like Eagles._

Jeremiah 29:11 - For I know the plans I have for you, declares the Lord, plans for welfare and not for evil, to give you a future and a hope.

1. What dreams, plans and purposes have you had that have been put on the shelf because of the busyness and distractions of your current **I** lifestyle?

2. Take time today to re-evaluate those dreams. Allow the Holy Spirit to stir and redirect you into His purposes as you learn to lay down those **I** distractions.

You are His Beloved!

A Life Lived On the Hamster Wheel? or Have You "Gone Fishing"?

As a type "A" personality I've spent most of my life seeing my life either as a juggler trying to keep all the plates spinning at the same time or as the constantly running hamster on the wheel. This was just who I was - or so I thought.

One day as my "people pleasing" "self imposed" spinning plates began to crash around me; I ranted out my frustration to God, hoping He would help me keep them going. However, that day I found that God has a sense of humor. In the midst of my tirade a minds eye picture flashed into my head. A painted board with the words "Gone Fishing" presented itself. My reaction quickly turned from startled to an uncontrollable laughter. I knew this was His direct answer to that prayer.

Embracing that thought, stopping the craziness, getting off the wheel, living it and walking it has taken me on a journey of finding the person I was designed to be.

In the resting and "going fishing" process, enjoyment of life begins to dawn as relief and freedom become possible. Trusting Jesus, His plan for your life and daily walking in a place of rest are all part of this growth.

Does everything get done? Nope. Does it matter? Nope. Do you lose friends? YES. Some of those you were constantly trying to please, those who kept you on the wheel due to their expectations but not ones that matter. Is it easy? Nope. Is it worth it? Oh Yes. It brings a clear focus of what is important in your life, brings new meaning and crystallizes your focus on who you were designed to be.

Join me in this amazing process. Get off the wheel. Take time to embrace, rest, and trust in Christ's unique design that is who you are. Enjoy going fishing.

<u>Day 1</u>

Spend some time contemplating what <u>*A Life Lived On the Hamster Wheel? Or Have You "Gone Fishing"?*</u> means to you.

1. What does this mean to you?

2. How does it apply to your life?

Day 2

John 10:10 - The thief comes only to steal and kill and destroy. I came that they may have life and have it abundantly.

Romans 8:1 - There is therefore now no condemnation for those who are in Christ Jesus.

1. Do you live a life of abundance filled with joy, peace and rest or one of juggling, plate spinning and people pleasing?

2. Knowing that all redirection in life comes from the loving hand of God and that there is no condemnation for a "re-start" in any area of our lives, evaluate and list where you see places that you can "get off the hamster wheel".

<u>Day 3</u>

Matthew 11:28-30 - Come to me, all who labor and are heavy laden, and I will give you rest. Take my yoke upon you, and learn from me, for I am gentle and lowly in heart, and you will find rest for your souls. For my yoke is easy, and my burden is light.

1. Learning to say <u>No</u> is a big part in this process. What specific things have you recently said yes to that you would have been better off to say no?

2. Apply the <u>No</u> process this week and note your feelings.

(If this is new to you, try responding to those who want your yes by saying "I will get back to you"; this will give you time to regroup, re-evaluate the request and make a response that is best fit for your life.)

Day 4

Proverbs 12:25 - Anxiety in a man's heart weighs him down, but a good word makes him glad.

Isaiah 26:3 - You keep him in perfect peace whose mind is stayed on you, because he trusts in you.

1. How would the process of "Gone Fishing" (resting in His Presence) change your life, bringing relief and freedom?

2. List some of those changes in the following areas:
   - i. Physically?
   - ii. Emotionally?
   - iii. Socially?
   - iv. Spiritually?

Day 5

Matthew 6:25-34 - Therefore I tell you, do not be anxious about your life, what you will eat or what you will drink, nor about your body, what you will put on. Is not life more than food, and the body more than clothing? Look at the birds of the air: they neither sow nor reap nor gather into barns, and yet your heavenly Father feeds them. Are you not of more value than they? And which of you by being anxious can add a single hour to his span of life? And why are you anxious about clothing? Consider the lilies of the field, how they grow: they neither toil nor spin, yet I tell you, even Solomon in all his glory was not arrayed like one of these. But if God so clothes the grass of the field, which today is alive and tomorrow is thrown into the oven, will he not much more clothe you, O you of little faith? Therefore do not be anxious, saying, 'What shall we eat?' or 'What shall we drink?' or 'What shall we wear?''

For the Gentiles seek after all these things, and your heavenly Father knows that you need them all.

But seek first the kingdom of God and his righteousness, and all these things will be added to you. Therefore do not be anxious about tomorrow, for tomorrow will be anxious for itself. Sufficient for the day is its own trouble.

1. How can embracing this scripture help as you adjust your life to the "Gone Fishing" lifestyle?

<u>Day 6</u>

Re-read <u>*A Life Lived On the Hamster Wheel? Or Have You "Gone Fishing"?*</u>.

Philippians. 1:6 - And I am sure of this, that he who began a good work in you will bring it to completion at the day of Jesus Christ.

This process has just begun. Remember that it is a journey whose fruit will become evident as you walk it out.

The distractions and busyness of your life may have disrupted your own purposes and unique design.

1. Spend time contemplating what those purposes and design look like. What new thoughts about your uniqueness have been stirred this week?

2. Take quiet time today to just sit in the Presence of our King. Listen to His voice and allow a thankful heart to stir a desire for more time to "Go Fishing" with Him.

You are righteous!

Go To The Mountain vs Go To The Mattresses

We all have a tendency to either go to the mountain or go to the mattresses as decisions are made in our lives.

Both mean you are preparing for a new direction, purpose, plan or battle. You are willing to risk it all to get there. It's just the approach that varies and that approach transforms you.

Which do you lean toward?

Both Jesus and Moses went to the Mountain.

Both were seeking strength, encouragement and direction for the task ahead.

Jesus met with Elijah and Moses, who prepared him for what was to come, their presence brought strength, encouragement and Gods manifest presence. This encounter transformed him for the task ahead.

Moses also, went to the Mountain seeking direction, strength and a manifest face to face encounter with God. He became stubborn, waiting for more! But that tenacity paid off and he was strengthened, prepared and transformed for His destiny.

During times of decision, change of direction and hard battles do you go to the Mountain? OR Go it on your own and go to the Mattresses?

As in an old saying used by the mafia in Italy – "going to the mattresses" means you will stand your ground – fight for your cause with all you have, with no restraint. Going to the Mattresses says YOU can do it - <u>you go into this on your own strength, knowledge and ingenuity</u> (leaving the direction of the Holy Spirit out of the equation).

Here YOU do it all; it takes all of you and usually will drain you to below <u>empty.</u> This will bring you to a place of stress, frustration and pressure. All in all, it is a very nasty place for you and for those who are still standing around you.

You say, "Yeah, but I'm not Jesus or Moses" - true, but you have the same choice and access to the throne of God.

You can head to the Mountain! You can wait there (sometimes wait a long time) and allow the Holy Spirit to meet with you. He will pour out on you his peace, direction and encouragement; preparing you for the task ahead. He can prepare you up on that Mountain versus doing it yourself down on the Mattresses (where you really need a chance to stop and collapse when or if you make it out the other end).

You will still have the decisions and work to be done when you come down from the Mountain.

However, you have been prepared for the task and the approach and ultimate out-come is totally different.

My Choice is to Go To The Mountain!

He will overshadow me and give me a peace filled transformation for the coming journey.

Each time you encounter that cross roads you have the choice too.

Take a minute the next time and decide if you want to Go to the Mountain or Go to the Mattresses.

Day 1

Spend some time contemplating what _Go To The Mountain vs Go To The Mattresses_ means to you.

1. What does this mean to you?

2. How does it apply to your life?

Day 2

Matthew 17:1-3 - And after six days Jesus took with him Peter and James, and John his brother, and led them up a high mountain by themselves. And he was transfigured before them, and his face shone like the sun, and his clothes became white as light. And behold, there appeared to them Moses and Elijah, talking with him.

Exodus 33:12-23 - Moses said to the LORD, "See, you say to me, 'Bring up this people,' but you have not let me know whom you will send with me. Yet you have said, 'I know you by name, and you have also found favor in my sight.' Now therefore, if I have found favor in your sight, please show me now your ways, that I may know you in order to find favor in your sight. Consider too that this nation is your people." And he said, "My presence will go with you, and I will give you rest." And he said to him, "If your presence will not go with me, do not bring us up from here. For how shall it be known that I have found favor in your sight, I and your people? Is it not in your going with us, so that we are distinct, I and your people, from every other people on the face of the earth?"And the LORD said to Moses, "This very thing that you have spoken I will do, for you have found favor in my sight, and I know you by name." Moses said, "Please show me your glory."

And he said, "I will make all my goodness pass before you and will proclaim before you my name 'The LORD.' And I will be gracious to whom I will be gracious, and will show mercy on whom I will show mercy. But," he said, "you cannot see my face, for man shall not see me and live." And the LORD said, "Behold, there is a place by me where you shall stand on the rock, and while my glory passes by I will put you in a cleft of the rock, and I will cover you with my hand until I have passed by. Then I will take away my hand, and you shall see my back, but my face shall not be seen."

1. In times of decision do you go to the mountain or go to the mattresses?

2. List one decision you made by going it on your own and the result.

3. List one decision you made by waiting on God's direction and the result.

Day 3

Philippians 4:6-7 - do not be anxious about anything, but in everything by prayer and supplication with thanksgiving let your requests be made known to God. And the peace of God, which surpasses all understanding, will guard your hearts and your minds in Christ Jesus.

1. Using this scripture - how can you apply the "going to the mountain" step to a decision you are currently facing?

2. Take time today to lay those decisions at His feet in prayer.

Day 4

Proverbs 3: 5-6 - Trust in the LORD with all your heart, and do not lean on your own understanding. In all your ways acknowledge him, and he will make straight your paths.

Psalm 26.1 - Vindicate me, O LORD, for I have walked in my integrity, and I have trusted in the LORD without wavering.

1. Learning to leave decisions at His feet is not always easy. Answers don't come over night, as with Moses. There are times you may need to stand and not waver. The above two scriptures are good ones to memorize for those waiting times. Spend time today memorizing them.

Day 5

Zechariah 4:6 - Then he said to me, "This is the word of the LORD to Zerubbabel: Not by might, nor by power, but by my Spirit, says the LORD of hosts.

1. What situations and decisions have you been "doing it on your own strength – on the mattresses" and have grown weary?

2. Make some reverse decisions today and head to the mountain for your strength. Spend time in His presence.

Day 6

Re-read *Go To The Mountain vs Go To The Mattresses*.

Psalm 16:11 - You make known to me the path of life; in your presence there is fullness of joy; at your right hand are pleasures forevermore.

1. Contemplate in prayer and determine today that as the cross roads of your life are encountered you will head to the mountain from which comes your strength. Write out your own confession of faith regarding what the Holy Spirit revealed during this time.

You are Holy!

The Seasons of Our Lives

A Different Way of Thinking

(Part 1 – Fall)

A recent read of a traditional thought regarding our lives and the seasons we go through caused my mind to do a double take and a new thinking began to emerge.

Our lives do mirror the seasons of nature, true - but I don't believe it is like we have thought. A cycle, yes - but a cycle that can be active and repeat in our lives sometimes daily, weekly, yearly and for varying time frames. The repetition of these cycles is part of life.

When we allow the flow of the seasons to have complete control we walk in a new understanding of what "being led by the Spirit" is really about. It's all about listening and moving from one season to the next when He speaks.

I love the Fall - so lets start there.

In nature it's a time of slowing down. Flowers have finished their spectacular display, trees have completed their fruiting purposes while squirrels and other gatherers are focused on one thing - preparation for the next season.

For us the Fall is a time of <u>simplification</u>, where we begin pulling all distractions away and focus becomes pinpoint - directed to His plan.

It's a time of preparation. This time can be for today's directed project or for an extended period as we wait for an appointed time of action.

This time of simplification requires you to make a choice. It is a choice to stop and pull away all the extra busyness you have accumulated. Prepare for His purpose and plan for your life by allowing empty time to exist.

It requires extensive time where you are content to sit at His feet and learn to rest and listen as He speaks.

Join me in this place of learning to simplify your life in preparation for His call.

Day 1

Spend some time contemplating what *The Seasons of Our Lives – A Different Way of Thinking (Part 1 - Fall)* means to you.

1. What does this mean to you?

2. How does it apply to your life?

Day 2

Psalm 27:4 - One thing have I asked of the Lord, that will I seek after: that I may dwell in the house of the Lord all the days of my life, to gaze upon the beauty of the Lord and to inquire in his temple."

Simplifying our lives can be a complicated decision. Making that choice with <u>one thing</u> in mind allows a peace to manifest within your spirit that satisfies beyond any activity. That <u>one thing</u> is the face of Jesus and His presence.

1. How can you apply simplification to your life today?

2. Since we can walk out the **Fall** season process daily or be in it for an extended time frame; where do you see this cycle working in your life?

Day 3

John 15:1-5 - I am the true vine, and my Father is the vinedresser. Every branch in me that does not bear fruit he takes away, and every branch that does bear fruit he prunes, that it may bear more fruit. Already you are clean because of the word that I have spoken to you. Abide in me, and I in you. As the branch cannot bear fruit by itself, unless it abides in the vine, neither can you, unless you abide in me. I am the vine; you are the branches. Whoever abides in me and I in him, he it is that bears much fruit, for apart from me you can do nothing.

1. How does this scripture apply to the process of simplification that we find in the Fall?

2. Spend time today abiding in His presence.

Day 4

Psalm 145:15-16 - The eyes of all look to you, and you give them their food in due season. You open your hand; you satisfy the desire of every living thing.

1. Look at nature and list how God provides specifically for each listed living thing.

2. Contemplate God's provision for the needs of nature and how much more He loves you who were created in His image. Make a choice today to trust and rest in His provision.

Day 5

As the creatures in nature prepare for winters rest we too can prepare for the next adventure that the Lord is directing in our lives. Doing that only as and when He directs; and knowing that He is the one to provide allows this preparation to be done in peace and not a "scurry" hurried attitude. Trust and knowledge of HIS provision is a must.

Isaiah 55:1 - Come, everyone who thirsts, come to the waters; and he who has no money, come, buy and eat! Come, buy wine and milk without money and without price.

1. In what areas of your life is the Lord directing some preparation?

2. Do you see yourself making those preparations in a scurry hurried attitude or one of rest?

Day 6

Re-read *The Seasons of Our Lives – A Different Way of Thinking (Part 1 – Fall)*.

Psalm 81:10 - I am the Lord your God, who brought you up out of the land of Egypt. Open your mouth wide, and I will fill it.

The Fall process may be a cycle that you walk through daily, yearly or a life process. Enjoy the journey with Jesus. Learning to simplify and trust Him allows your ears and eyes to be open to new directions. Remember - if He directs it – He is faithful to complete it. Open your mouth wide and He will fill it.

1. Take time today to sit in His presence, rest and listen.

2. Make one decision today that will simplify your life - (simple or major as the Lord directs) and implement it.

3. Journal the God thoughts that began to surface today as you waited in His presence.

You are loved!

The Seasons of Our Lives

A Different Way of Thinking

(Part 2 – Winter)

I look at winter differently too.

What's winter in nature? It's a quiet time, a time of active rest and peace.

Active rest because a lot happens in those quiet underground-unseen places of nature. During this quiet time strength is infused to all types of roots. It's a time of multiplication. Life is being conceived both in wildlife as well as bulbs and seeds. These are all examples of natures expected growth to come.

For us, I don't see it as a <u>dark night of the soul</u> or <u>suffering that God puts us through</u>. NO WAY! Not my Jesus!

During this time for us it's a time for wheels to stop turning. The "I can do" lays down to rest in what "He did".

It's a time for us to sit at His feet, gather strength, learn to wait and trust His plan for each day and for our life.

It's a time of expectant multiplication as we rest and wait. This can be an hour in our day or years - it's all about His timing.

Day 1

Spend some time contemplating what *The Seasons of our Lives – A Different Way of Thinking (Part 2-Winter)* means to you.

1. What does this mean to you?

2. How does it apply to your life?

Day 2

Romans 8:19 - For the creation waits with eager longing for the revealing of the sons of God.

1. How would you describe the term "active rest"?

2. As creation eagerly waits so do we. Knowing that Jesus already did it all for you - do you still struggle with areas of "I can do it"? If so how can you let them go?

Day 3

Psalm 62:1 - For God alone my soul waits in silence; from him comes my salvation.

Psalm 62:5 - For God alone, O my soul, wait in silence, for my hope is from him.

Learning to sit in silence is a major chore in this never unplugged society.   It takes an honest concerted effort to accomplish it.

1. Spend 15 min. today in a waiting - **silent** posture before the Lord.

   Don't get discouraged when your mind begins to run over your to do list at minute 5 - breath and start again.   It will become a lifestyle of silence that you will learn to gain amazing strength from as this new discipline brings you daily into His presence.

2. Journal your thoughts of this process as well as any God thoughts that He may have spoken during this time of silence.

Day 4

Colossians 3:15 - And let the peace of Christ rule in your hearts, to which indeed you were called in one body. And be thankful.

John 14:1 - Let not your hearts be troubled. Believe in God; believe also in me.

1. Yesterday we implemented a discipline of silence. What <u>busy</u> thoughts kept jumping into your <u>silent</u> space?

2. In Christ we are designed and promised a life of peace that will rule in our hearts. Today write down all those **busy** thoughts that are demanding your attention right now. THEN lay them aside and try again today to sit in His presence.

3. Journal any God thoughts that stirred as you waited in silence.

Day 5

Isaiah 30:15 - For thus said the Lord GOD, the Holy One of Israel, "In returning and rest you shall be saved; in quietness and in trust shall be your strength."

Isaiah 41:10 - Fear not, for I am with you; be not dismayed, for I am your God; I will strengthen you, I will help you, I will uphold you with my righteous right hand.

He promises us strength. Walking through a winter cycle is a time of learning His promises, allowing Him to strengthen us and to quietly wait with active peaceful anticipation of His plans and purposes for our life.

1. What areas in your life need some strength today?

2. Enjoy your **silent** time today as you meditate specifically on His promise for strength.

3. Journal your thoughts from your **silent** time.

<u>Day 6</u>

Re-read <u>*The Seasons of Our Lives – A Different Way of*</u> <u>*Thinking (Part 2 – Winter)*</u>.

Isaiah 32:18 - My people will abide in a peaceful habitation, in secure dwellings, and in quiet resting places.

1. How has the implementation of a discipline of silence in His presence brought peace, rest and strength this week?

You are righteous!

The Seasons of Our Lives
A Different Way of Thinking
(Part 3 – Spring)

Spring emerges from winters rest and with it a new hope and an explosion of energy - creating new life for all of nature.

The trees bud, flowers bloom and babies are born.

As you feel, smell and hear spring approach something within your very being begins to stir. It's a promise of new life that is ignited by the very emergence of the small internal voice saying "Yes" and "Amen" to the Creators' promises.

You begin to have new directions, new visions, renewed hope, new strength and energy to drive forward that which you are hearing His voice proclaim over your life.

During this spring stirring take time to journal all the exciting thoughts, questions, directions and plans that He has been speaking into your spirit during winters rest. These will begin to bloom as you lay them at His feet and wait for His directions.

Rejoice in the His assurance of His love and plans for you.

Day 1

Spend some time contemplating what _The Seasons of our Lives – A Different Way of Thinking (Part 3 - Spring)_ means to you.

1. What does this mean to you?

2. How does it apply to your life?

Day 2

2 Corinthians 1:20 - For all the promises of God find their Yes in him. That is why it is through him that we utter our Amen to God for his glory.

1. What specific promises from the Bible do you feel the Holy Spirit is speaking into your life to stand on and believe for?

2. Spend time today meditating on the above scripture and rejoice in the multitude of promises in the Word that He has given to you.

Day 3

Isaiah 55:10-11 - For as the rain and the snow come down from heaven and do not return there but water the earth, making it bring forth and sprout, giving seed to the sower and bread to the eater, so shall my word be that goes out from my mouth; it shall not return to me empty, but it shall accomplish that which I purpose, and shall succeed in the thing for which I sent it.

1. List some areas in your life that have been "sleeping" – but now God is beginning to stir them up within you.

2. Enjoy time in His presence listening to his directions for waking up those sleeping visions and dreams. Take time to journal those thoughts.

Day 4

Psalm 20:4 - May he grant you your heart's desire and fulfill all your plans!

1. Thinking outside of the box - what would you love to do if there was nothing holding you back?

2. What specifics would be required to step out of that box?

Spend time sitting with the Lord today. Bring the above thoughts to Him and see what His direction might be.

Day 5

Spring erupts with the sound of praise from every creature. Just as the birds sing out with praise - a thankful heart within us restores new life.

Psalm 95:2 - Let us come into his presence with thanksgiving; let us make a joyful noise to him with songs of praise!

1. List at least five things you are thankful for today and the impact they have on your life.

2. Worship with a new found freedom today.

Day 6

Re-read *The Seasons of Our Lives – A Different Way of Thinking (Part 3 – Spring).*

2 Timothy 2:1 - You then, my child, be strengthened by the grace that is in Christ Jesus.

    1. As you have walked through this week - what promises in the Word are finding their "Yes" and "Amen" within you?

    2. What does it mean to be "strengthened by the grace that is Christ Jesus"?

REJOICE in the gift of grace you have received – unmerited favor!

You are a child of the KING!

The Seasons of Our Lives
A Different Way of Thinking
(Part 4 - Summer)

Then comes summer; we all love summer! Nature and man alike can bask with all of our senses as creation vibrates with life.

Nature gets her opportunity to show off to us as she produces beautiful flowers, foliage, fruits and nuts. She orchestrates songs of rejoicing from wildlife. She energizes movement of waters as well as the radiating warmth of the sun. Fresh breezes that breathe through the trees and flowers are all part of her expression. All of our senses come alive as we partake in her offerings. Her amazing aromas, unspeakable displays of beauty, and warming sunrays seep deep into our lives. Her refreshing breezes and scrumptious flavors of fresh produce tantalize our senses.

For us summer brings times of great enjoyment.

Fruitfulness as His favor and abundant provision is poured out on all that we put our hand to.

This cycle can be enjoyed daily or as often as you are blessed with it.

The gift of summer truly is meant by God to be a gift to His children. He desires His kids to have fun and take time to lean back and relax.

He already paid for this vacation. It's an all expenses paid gift from His son Jesus. Just accept it and know that it's ok to enjoy summer and walk in life filled with continual refreshment.

Day 1

Spend some time contemplating what _The Seasons of our Lives – A Different Way of Thinking (Part 4 – Summer)_ means to you.

1. What does this mean to you?

2. How does it apply to your life?

Day 2

Psalm 84:11-12 - For the Lord God is a sun and shield; the Lord bestows favor and honor. No good thing does he withhold from those who walk uprightly. O Lord of hosts, blessed is the one who trusts in you.

1. Journal about a time of specific abundant provision and how you felt.

2. In what areas of your life do you see Gods favor and abundant provision operating today?

Day 3

There are summer times to experience in all of our lives. Looking for them and being thankful produces a heart that will sing throughout every situation.

Psalm 1:3 - He is like a tree planted by streams of water that yields its fruit in its season, and its leaf does not wither. In all that he does, he prospers.

1. What are you thankful for today?

2. Take time today to draw refreshment from the streams of living water in your secret place at the feet of Jesus and journal your thoughts.

Day 4

Joy springs forth from those who walk daily in His presence.

John 7:37-38 - On the last day of the feast, the great day, Jesus stood up and cried out, "If anyone thirsts, let him come to me and drink. Whoever believes in me, as the Scripture has said, 'Out of his heart will flow rivers of living water.'"

    1. How do you know if you are thirsty for the presence of Jesus?

    2. When, where and how do you "go to Him to drink"?

Day 5

Psalm 13:5-6 - But I have trusted in your steadfast love; my heart shall rejoice in your salvation. I will sing to the LORD, because he has dealt bountifully with me.

1. Which cycle of the seasons do you feel you are currently in?

2. How do you know? What specifics are you experiencing that point you to that conclusion?

3. Embrace it. Rejoice and rest where He has you.

Day 6

Re-read *The Seasons of Our Lives – A Different Way of Thinking (Part 4 – Summer)*.

All that God has for us is summed up in the cycle of the seasons of our lives. His plan is always for the best of each season to be embraced and enjoyed. So relax, don't struggle and strive or wish you were in another season. Nature doesn't; we do well to observe and understand that. It's a journey of peace if we just decide to get off the wheel and take His hand to walk the amazing trails He has planned for us.

No one has the same trail so don't try to jump or run ahead to catch up with another. Just rest and allow your cycle to have its completion in you and remember to enjoy your walk with Jesus. He is faithful to complete what He has started.

Psalm 92: 1-4 - It is good to give thanks to the LORD, to sing praises to your name, O Most High; to declare your steadfast love in the morning, and your faithfulness by night, to the music of the lute and the harp, to the melody of the lyre. For you, O LORD, have made me glad by your work; at the works of your hands I sing for joy.

1. We often need to find summer experiences in our lives – setting time aside and planning fun activities. These times bring refreshment – mentally, physically and spiritually.
Take time today to implement this thought.

You are highly favored!

Cinderella and the Bride of Christ

As children we fall in love with the fairy tales of Princesses and Princes. Little girls become women with the "Cinderella syndrome" buried in their hearts. Little boys become men looking to rescue their "one true love".

Why is that so deep within us?

I think that somewhere inside of all of us is the hope that there is truth in those stories. So, lets look at this differently for a moment.

Our prince, Jesus will come. He is waiting to return for His bride and to whisk her away to His magic kingdom with streets of gold and crystal waters for all eternity.

Cinderella was born into nobility yet was forced into servitude. She lived where evil prevailed daily and was treated as evil by her own family members. So happens to us - the Bride of Christ.

She IS noble but her true identity has been covered over with the thinking and distractions of this world. Buried like a charwoman who is covered with soot, grime and ash this once beautiful noble bride has lost sight of her one true love.

The Bible says that our prince is returning for a Bride that has made herself ready.

Just as Cinderella had a secret place that sustained her, a place of joy that welled up within her, a place that brought songs erupting from within and brought change to her heart; so must the Bride of Christ find that secret place where the face of Jesus is the <u>one thing</u> that matters. Then her identity will shine through, her hopelessness will begin to fall away and she will erupt with joy that will change the very atmosphere around her.

As with Cinderella, the favor will present itself and in an instant the change from scullery maid to Bride will occur. Her eyes will be only for her prince. All else will fade away. His return on a white horse to whisk her away to the magic kingdom is eminent.

Let's find that secret place and focus only on the face of our beloved. Let's be the Bride that has made herself ready. Let's have our hand on the door ready when our prince rides up on his white horse with glass slipper in hand. Let's rejoice in knowing that He has come for us!

Day 1

Spend some time contemplating what _Cinderella and The Bride of Christ_ means to you.

1. What does this mean to you?

2. How does it apply to your life?

Day 2

Knowing our true identity in Christ will release us from performance and allow us to get off the hamster wheel of life.

He chose you, loves you and desires you to sit at His feet. Just as a bridegroom has eyes only for his bride so are the eyes of Jesus only for you - His beloved. There is nothing you can do to increase that love or to diminish it. His love is a gift that is free of charge. He says, "Come".

Revelation 22:17 - The Spirit and the Bride say, "Come." And let the one who hears say, "Come." And let the one who is thirsty come; let the one who desires take the water of life without price.

1. How is your identity in Christ becoming clearer to you?

2. Do you find your heart being tugged to "Come" and sit in His presence more often?

3. How can you adjust your life to allow time to run into that secret place when that call comes?

Day 3

Not allowing our lives to be covered in soot, grime and ash only can occur because our eyes are focused on the <u>one thing</u> the gift of love given at the cross by the poured out blood of Jesus. We can't be clean on our own. Our works and achievements are but dirty rags. His blood changes our best-planned bridal garment from rags into a glorious one of pure white.

Hebrews 10:23 - Let us hold fast the confession of our hope without wavering, for he who promised is faithful.

1. What is your personal confession of the hope you have?

2. Meditate on His gift of grace and forgiveness given for you. Journal a time that you have stood up for your belief in Christ and how you felt during and after that experience.

Day 4

Walking in the favor and grace of Christ doesn't mean we sit and do nothing. However, the key to active rest can only be found by learning to sit, rest and listen. His presence is where your lamps are refilled with the oil of the Holy Spirit. Only then can your heart be available to hear from the Holy Spirit as He directs you to move into what His plans and purposes are for your life.

Luke 12:35-37 - Stay dressed for action and keep your lamps burning, and be like men who are waiting for their master to come home from the wedding feast, so that they may open the door to him at once when he comes and knocks.

1. What does it mean to you to "stay dressed for action and keep your lamp burning"?

2. During the last 3 months how is your life being re-directed to a place of "keeping your lamp burning"?

Day 5

2 Corinthians 2:15-17 - For we are the aroma of Christ to God among those who are being saved and among those who are perishing, to one a fragrance from death to death, to the other a fragrance from life to life. Who is sufficient for these things? For we are not, like so many, peddlers of God's word, but as men of sincerity, as commissioned by God, in the sight of God we speak in Christ.

What an amazing assignment – to be the aroma of God. As we walk daily in our true identity as a child of the King the very atmosphere around us changes. It's not by our diligent "doing it" as we beat people over the head with the Bible but by allowing His love to pour out of us like suave over broken and torn flesh. Then our aroma will be that of Christ and will transform our atmosphere and those around us.

1. Do you know who God has designed you to be? Rejoice in that! Don't try to "fit" into someone else's shoes.

2. What assignment do you feel God has
   recently given you?

Spend time today praying into that and listening
to His directions.

Day 6

Re-read *Cinderella and The Bride of Christ*.

Song of Solomon 6:3 - I am my beloved's and my beloved is mine; he grazes among the lilies.

1. Spend some time today journaling your thoughts comparing the needs, desires and actions that a bride and groom have in our current society - to us as the bride of Christ and Christ as our bridegroom.

2. How can you keep your eyes focused on the bridegroom?

<u>Allow your song of joy to erupt from within.</u>

You are His Beloved!

Titles available by J.K. Sanchez

Majestic Reflection Devotional Study Series:

Winters Rest

Spring's Assurance

Summer's Delight

Fall's Yield

Stand alone or companion journals:

Winters Rest Journal

Spring's Assurance Journal

Summer's Delight Journal

Fall's Yield Journal

Majestic Reflection Journal

Reflections of His Glory Journal

Additional Titles

Reflections of His Glory

Contact me at: Judy@jksanchez.com

Jksanchez.com

Also find me on Amazon.com

About the Author

J. K. Sanchez has lived and raised her three children in the Pacific Northwest where she and her husband of 40 years live and enjoy its beauty. As a writer and photographer her love of nature has flourished and is portrayed both through visually descriptive prose as well as through the eye of the camera.

Having ministered in many areas of the body of Christ her love for people and passion for worship and the presence of the Lord continually draw her to see freedom proclaimed and released to others through the finished work on the cross of Jesus.

<u>Notes</u>

Notes